The Doctrine of Man's Future Eternity
by John Jackson
with chapters by C. Matthew McMahon

Copyright Information

The Doctrine of Man's Future Eternity, by John Jackson, with chapters by C. Matthew McMahon
Edited by Susan Ruth and Therese B. McMahon

Copyright ©2020 by Puritan Publications and A Puritan's Mind

Some language and grammar have been updated from the original manuscript. Any change in wording or punctuation has not changed the intent or meaning of the original author(s), and has been made to aid the modern reader.

Published by Puritan Publications
A Ministry of A Puritan's Mind ®
Crossville, TN
www.puritanpublications.com
www.apuritansmind.com

All rights reserved. No part of this publication may be reproduced, stored in a retrieval system or transmitted in any form by any means, electronic, mechanical, photocopy, recording or otherwise, without the prior permission of the publisher, except as provided by USA copyright law.

Manufactured in the United States of America

eISBN: 978-1-62663-374-2
ISBN: 978-1-62663-375-9

Table of Contents

Jackson Weighs Eternity in the Balance 4

Meet John Jackson 7

Dedication 11

Chapter 1: Six Principles 12

Chapter 2: Happiness or Misery 22

Chapter 3: Misery of the Wicked 30

Chapter 4: Glory for the Righteous 43

Chapter 5: Bodies and Souls 62

Chapter 6: Application of the Doctrine 68

Other Books on Heaven and Hell Published by Puritan Publications 97

Jackson Weighs Eternity in the Balance

by C. Matthew McMahon, Ph.D., Th.D.

Jackson's works are often simple, but penetrating, while at the same time biblically insightful. As a preacher, he always had in mind the benefit of the hearer, or in this case, *the reader*, in those things which he taught. In this work he actually takes that task to another degree by pressing and exhorting the reader, speaking to them directly, to make the most of the principles he lays down concerning eternity, and the never dying soul that hangs in its balance. He believed, and rightly so, that such a doctrine taught by the Old Testament and New Testament abundantly appears how necessary it is that this fundamental point of divinity (of man's future eternity) should be "plainly proved, clearly explained, and powerfully applied to us."

In this work, Jackson explains the six principles surrounding the estate of all mankind until the end of this world, by way of preface to the proof of the doctrine concerning man's eternity in the world to come. He shows what eternity is in the final four basic tenants of Christian doctrine, death, judgment, heaven and hell.

He then proves by Scripture the many infallible proofs that all mankind, at the end of this world, shall go in their bodies and souls into an *everlasting condition,* either of happiness or misery. Which one will you go to reader? How can you be sure of your eternal destination in which you will remain forever in both body and soul?

Next, he describes the *misery* of that everlasting condition of woe and punishment that the wicked shall go into at the end of the world. He explains cogently the Scriptural doctrine of eternal misery in hell, and presses the reader to consider the truth of Christ's preaching, and the bible's teaching, of eternity in light of God's wrath and punishment.

Then, he goes on to explain the happiness of the eternal state of glory and rest that the righteous shall go into at the last day. This is a most excellent and comforting exhortation to understand the eternal felicity that the saints have after death.

Next, he takes a chapter to explain the principal reasons why all mankind after the day of judgment shall go in their bodies and souls into an everlasting condition, either of happiness or misery. This is very important chapter, in that, he not only has stated the biblical case, but then refers the reader to contemplate *why* it is the case; why going, body and soul, into eternity, is the height of importance for all people to consider *now* before they die, when such considerations after they die will be too late.

In the last chapter he directs the reader how to apply the great doctrine of man's future eternity, by which you (reader) may escape everlasting punishment, and obtain life eternal in Christ, after this life is ended. This application is the longest part of the work, pressing the reader to discern where they are going, and how they can make the most of their time while here on earth in order to be *sure* of their calling and election. Jackson desired that the reader escape the horrible and miserable eternal death that awaits them if they are not found in Christ.

This is a blessed work, short in its stature, but deep in its power and application. A God-glorifying and Christ exalting work by this eminent divine.

In the Grace of Christ,
C. Matthew McMahon, Ph.D., Th.D.
From my study, August, 2020.

Meet John Jackson
by C. Matthew McMahon, Ph.D., Th.D.

Information on John Jackson (1600-1648) is scarce. However, the following is the best compilation of information found on him from both history books and current biographies.

Jackson was born in 1600, one of 3 brothers, possibly in Melsonby, North Riding of Yorkshire, and matriculated to Christ's college in July of 1613. He earned his B.A. in 1616 and his M.A. in 1620. He seems to have gone to Lincoln College in Oxford on June 7, 1616. During this time he became Master of Richmond Grammar School in North Riding in 1618 and remained at that post for two years. This school was ten miles from his birthplace and perhaps where he himself had studied.[1] After his conversion he became a deacon on December 19, 1619 and then a minister of the Gospel in February 1623. In 1623 he took over the rectory of Marske in North Riding of Yorkshire, and consequently also of Barwick-in-Elmet, which was in West Riding of Yorkshire. He married the daughter of Ralph Bowes of St. Mary-le-

---

[1] Al. *Cant.* II, 445; Bartholomew's *Survey Atlas*, p. 74.

Bow, Durham, on October 13, 1629, and from 1642-1644 was preacher at Gray's Inn.[2]

In Daniel Neal's *Puritans*, he is mentioned in the list of the Assembly of Divines who met at Westminster as *John Jackson, A.M. of Queen's college, Cambridge*. Wood mentions several persons of the name (such as John Jackson, M.A. of Cambridge, it seems, born in Lancashire, beneficed in Essex, and author of several tracts of practical divinity).

Jackson is named in the ordinance of the Parliament for calling an Assembly of learned and godly divines. He is said to be *John Jackson of Marske*. Jackson is represented as constantly attending the Assembly during their sessions.

Though Jackson was a thorough puritan, he was a royalist; *i.e.* a supporter of the king as head of state.

Jackson retired to Barwick (which was West Riding of Yorkshire) on the arraignment of the King. He died in 1648 and was buried Barwick on January 22.

His works are the following:

---

[2] Wood's *Athena Oxon.* vol. i. *Fasti*, p. 279. 2d edit.

1. He wrote the dedicatory epistle to *The Morall Law expounded*, etc. written by Lancelot Andrewes. 4to. 1642.
2. "The Booke of Conscience opened and read." In a sermon on Prov. 15:15 preached at the Spittle on Easter Tuesday. 12vo. London, 1642.
3. A sermon on "Ecclesiastes. The worthy Church-Man," London, 1628.
4. "The Key of Knowledge," London, 1640.
5. "The True Evangelical Temper." Preached in three sermons at St. Martins in the Strand, upon the lucent Prophecie of Peace, and Union, Esay. chap. 11. v. 6, 7, and 8. 8vo. pp. 233. R. Milbourne: London, 1641.
6. "A Taste of the Truth as it is in Jesus," *etc.* 1648.
7. "The faithful Minister of Jesus Christ, described by polishing the twelve Stones in the High Priest's Pectoral, *etc.*" London, 1628. (Republished by Puritan Publications).
8. "A Treatise Concerning Man's Future Eternity; Wherein the great doctrine of eternity of all mankind in the world to come, either in happiness or misery, is proved, explained, and applied." 1661.

9. "A Sober Word to a Serious People," which deals with differences between churches.

Dedication

To the only honor and glory of God, and to the use and benefit of the people of England; and especially of his beloved parishioners, and worthy friends in Essex; and of his dear kindred, and respected countrymen in Lancashire.

John Jackson humbly dedicates this treatise to them concerning *man's future eternity*.

Chapter 1:
Six Principles

Six received principles about the estate of all mankind until the end of this world, by way of preface to the proof of the doctrine concerning man's eternity in the world to come.

Most of us are so exceedingly slow of heart to believe the great doctrine of the eternity of all mankind in the world to come, either in happiness or misery, and are extremely backward to provide for our own eternal condition. By this it abundantly appears how necessary it is that this fundamental point of divinity should be plainly proved, clearly explained, and powerfully applied to us.

But before I handle its particulars, I shall make an entrance to it by laying down six received principles concerning the estate of all mankind until the end of the world. For this purpose, that we may all *know ourselves*, and that we may clearly see how this infallible truth shall be fulfilled, in which we are all so nearly concerned.

1. First, that every one of mankind consists of a body and a soul joined together.

The Doctrine of Man's Future Eternity

The exhortation of Jesus Christ is, "Fear not them which kill the body, but are not able to kill the soul," and this plainly proves that every one of us has both a body and a soul, (Matthew 10:28). And these words of the Apostle Paul, "We have had fathers of our flesh, which corrected us, and we gave them reverence: shall we not much rather be in subjection to the Father of spirits?" (Hebrews 12:9) clearly imply that we had our bodies originally from our parents, the "fruit," (Psalm 132:11) of whose bodies, our bodies are. And that we had our souls originally from our God, who is said in holy Scripture to be the, "giver of them, and the God of the spirits of all flesh," (Numbers 16:22; Ecclesiastes 12:7).

It is probable that the Lord creates every particular soul, and that he infuses it into the body of an infant, when in all essential parts it is a perfect body, as Adam was, when God gave him his soul. This is the common opinion of modern writers[1] about the origin of the soul, and it is grounded upon those Scriptures where God is said to be the "Creator of the soul," and where the Lord is described as the "God, which formeth the spirit of man within him," (Isaiah 57:16, Zechariah 12:2, 1 Peter 4:19).

---

[1] See Bishop Reynolds' work *on the vanity of the creature.*

Chapter 1: Six Principles

2. Secondly, that the body of every one of mankind is mortal, subject to die daily, and that in many ways; some are no sooner born,[2] but they die, and those who have lived the longest lives, have died. As surely as we live in the body, so surely we must die in the body, and God knows how soon and how suddenly! "What man is he that liveth (the prophet David says) and shall not see death?" (Psalm 83:48). "For what is our life? It is but a vapor (the Apostle James says) that appeareth for a little time, and then vanisheth away," (James 4:14).

As the finer metal of any glass,[3] or earthen vessel is, the more subject it is to breaking, so, the daintiest bodies are soonest gone; and first or last, we must all die, because the Lord of life and death has appointed it, (Hebrews 9:27).

3. Thirdly, that the soul of every one of mankind is immortal, and no way liable to be killed; it neither dies with the body, nor sleeps in it: but immediately after the death of the body, the soul goes to God that gave it, to give it particular account, and to be judged either to go to heaven to be comforted, or else to go to hell to be tormented. So, that presently after death and particular

---

[2] Job 14:2; Genesis 5:5; 20:27.
[3] Mr. Strode's *Anatomy of Mortality*.

judgment, the soul enters into its endless eternity, either of comfort or torment. Solomon says when the body dies, "Then shall the dust return to the earth, as it was: and the spirit unto God who gave it," (Ecclesiastes 12:7). Our Savior says, "Fear not them that kill the body, but are not able to kill the soul," (Matthew 10:28). And Paul says, "It is appointed unto men once to die, and after this the judgment;" after death, judgment presently follows, as the Greek words signify,[4] and therefore by judgment here is meant (at least inclusively) that particular judgment which the Lord passes upon every soul immediately after death, for at that instant, God pronounces, and the conscience apprehends a sentence of blessing or cursing, and accordingly the soul is set in its eternal condition, either of felicity or misery.[5]

The souls of all those who die in the Lord,[6] in a believing and regenerate estate, are by the mercy of God absolved and made perfect in holiness, and are carried by good angels into heaven. There they live in a happy state of joy and rest, with their ever blessed God and Savior, and with all the holy angels, and with all those perfect

---

[4] Hebrews 9:27 compared with Job 5:4; 19:28.
[5] Bishop Ussher's *Body of Divinity*, p. 446.
[6] Revelation 14:13; Hebrews 12:23; Luke 16:22; 25; 23:43; Acts 7:59; Philippians 1:23.

and blessed souls who went to heaven before them. There they are waiting for the full redemption of their bodies, which even in death and after they are returned to dust, still continue united to Christ, and rest in their graves, as in their beds, until at the last day, they are again united to their souls, (Romans 8:23; Psalm 16:9; Isaiah 57:2; Job 19:25-26).

But the souls of all people who die out of Christ, in an unbelieving and unregenerate condition, are by the justice of God[7] condemned to infernal misery, and are hauled away by evil angels into hell, there to remain in torments and utter darkness with the devil and his angels, and with all those sad and miserable souls, who were before doomed to that place of torment. And their bodies which return to dust and see corruption, are kept in their grave, as in their prisons, until the resurrection and judgment of the great day, (Genesis 3:19; 2 Peter 2:9).

A philosopher being asked by Alexander the Great, "Whether there were more men alive than dead?"[8] Answered, "That there were more alive, because (he said) there are none dead in respect of their souls." We

---

[7] Ecclesiastes 12:7; Luke 12:20; 16:23-24; Acts 1:25; 1 Peter 3:19; Jude 6-7.
[8] P. Mor *de ver.* ch. Rel. c. 15.

are taught more plainly by divinity, than ever anywhere by philosophy, "That the souls of all people are immortal," and consequently that those who are dead in their bodies, are alive in their souls, either in heaven or hell. Besides these two places,[9] for souls separated from their bodies, the Scripture acknowledges none.

4. Fourthly, that the bodies of all mankind who have died from the beginning to the end of the world, shall all be raised again at the last day, and reunited to their own souls; all the dead shall be raised again with the same bodies, and no others, yet so altered in quality, as that, then, they shall be able to abide forever.

The words of our Savior are express and full in this matter, "The hour is coming, in the which all that are in the graves shall hear his voice, and shall come forth, they that have done good, unto the resurrection of life, and they that have done evil, unto the resurrection of damnation," (John 5:28-29). And the words of the Apostles are clear and plain, "There shall be a resurrection of the dead, both of the just and unjust," (Acts 24:15). And again, "The dead shall be raised incorruptible, and we shall be changed, for this

---

[9] Luke 16:23-24.

corruptible must put on incorruption, and this mortal must put on immortality," (1 Corinthians 15:52-53).

Do not let incredulous nature shrink at the possibility of the resurrection, when the God of nature undertakes it. Why should it be thought as an incredible thing that God should raise the dead? Is it not as possible for God Almighty (with whom nothing is impossible[10]) to raise the dead out of the dust, which is something like making the whole world out of nothing? Is it not as easy with the Lord (for whom nothing is too hard[11]) to raise man out of his dust in the earth, as to form man of the dust of the ground? It is sufficient to me that the Lord Jesus Christ has promised me that if I believe in him, he will raise me up at the last day, (John 6:40).

5. Fifthly, that all those of mankind who shall be raised from the dead, together with the rest of mankind, who shall be found alive at the second coming of Christ, "being changed in a moment," they shall all personally appear before the judgment seat of Christ to give a public account of their thoughts, words, and deeds, whether they were good or evil. And they shall all be judged by Jesus Christ to go in their actual bodies and

---

[10] Matthew 19:26.
[11] Jeremiah 32:17.

souls into an everlasting condition, either of happiness or misery.

Our Savior, in his sermons, often made mention of the Day of Judgment. Enoch, the seventh from Adam,[12] preached of this day of judgment. The Apostle Paul solemnly warns us of it.[13] Paul says, "We must all appear before the judgment seat of Christ, that everyone may receive the things done in his body according to that he hath done, whether it be good or bad; so then everyone shall give an account of himself to God, who will judge the secrets of men by Jesus Christ according to the Gospel, and will reward them according to their works," as their works or deeds were fruits and effects, either of their faith, or of their unbelief, (Matthew 16:27; Romans 2:6, 16).

Again, Matthew tells us that Jesus Christ, the Judge [14] of the quick and the dead, shall give this comfortable sentence of everlasting life and salvation to all the elect among mankind, who were righteous, and such as had a part in him; "Come ye blessed of my Father,

---

[12] Jude 14-15; Matthew 11:22, 24.
[13] 2 Corinthians 5:10; Romans 14:11; Ecclesiastes 12:14; 1 Corinthians 4:5.
[14] John 5:22; Acts 10:42.

inherit the kingdom prepared for you from the foundation of the world," (Matthew 25:34).

And again, that Christ himself shall give this dreadful sentence of eternal death and damnation to all the reprobate of mankind, who were wicked, and such as had no interest in him, "Depart from me ye cursed into everlasting fire, prepared for the devil and his angels," (Matthew 25:41).

It seems that the proceedings of the general and last judgment shall be so ordered by the peculiar favor of God, as that the saints who were in Christ shall first be judged and acquitted, and then with Christ, they shall judge reprobate men and angels, not in an equal authority with Christ, but as approvers of his righteous judgment.

6. Sixthly, that all mankind shall certainly go into that everlasting condition, that the Lord Jesus Christ shall doom them to. Those above whom Christ shall absolve, and sentence to inherit the kingdom of heaven, shall assuredly go into it, to live eternally happy in it. And those whom Christ shall condemn to go into everlasting fire, shall certainly go into it to be everlastingly punished in it; after the act of eternal

judgment is past, its execution will immediately follow; this is proved and insisted on in the next chapter.

Chapter 2:
Happiness or Misery

Showing by many infallible proofs that all mankind in the end of this world shall go in their bodies and souls into an everlasting condition, either of happiness or misery.

I have now brought you within the sight of man's future eternity, to that great doctrine of eternity chiefly aimed at, which is this, *that all mankind at the end of this world shall go in their bodies and souls to an everlasting condition, either of happiness or misery.* The wicked of all mankind, who had no part in Christ, shall go into hell, to endure everlasting punishment; and the righteous among all mankind, who were interested in Christ, shall go into heaven, to inherit life eternal. And so, all the world shall go into one of these two places or states of eternity, after that time shall be no more.

The truth of this weighty point of divinity may appear these two ways: by divine testimony or by human testimony.

1. First, this appears to be so by divine testimony of the Spirit of God in the holy Scriptures, who say

concerning the wicked, that they shall, "go into everlasting punishment, but the righteous into life eternal," (Matthew 25:46).

When Jesus Christ shall sit upon the throne of his glory, the people of all nations shall be gathered before him, and he will distinguish them into two sorts, namely into "sheep and goats," (Matthew 25:31-32). By goats are meant the reprobate of all mankind, who died in their sins,[1] and out of Christ: though many of them professed faith, yet none of them had that faith unfeigned, which works by love; for when Christ in his poor members was hungry, they gave him no meat, and when he was naked, they clothed him not; and these are the unbelieving and ungodly of the world, who shall go away into "everlasting punishment,"[2] that is, they shall go into hell to suffer everlasting punishment.

By sheep are to be understood the elect of God, taken out of all[3] sorts of mankind, who were redeemed, justified, and sanctified by Jesus Christ. Many of which had opportunity to show forth their faith in Christ, and their love to Christ, by their charity to the poor people of Christ. For, when Christ in his poor members was

---

[1] John 8:24; Luke 8:13; Hebrews 10:39; Matthew 25:42-43.
[2] *Metoniat adjuncti Piscator ad locum.*
[3] Revelation 5:9; 1 Corinthians 1:30; 2 Corinthians 6:11.

sick and in prison, they visited him, and when he was hungry and naked, they fed him, and clothed him. And these are the righteous in Christ Jesus, who shall go into life eternal,[4] that is, they shall go into heaven to enjoy eternal life, (Matthew 25:35-37, 46).

Again, this is proved by the parable of the tares of the field, in Matthew 13. If you observe well our Savior's exposition of this parable, you will find that all people in the world are compared to good seed or tares. By tares are meant the children of the wicked one, who were "of their father the devil, for his lusts they would do," (John 8:44; Titus 1:16); though many of them were Christians by name and believers by profession, yet they were but formal Christians, and feigned believers, being such as offended, and such as were workers of iniquity; And these in the end of this world, shall be cast into a furnace of fire; that is, into hellfire, where there is forever "wailing and gnashing of teeth," (Matthew 13:40-42; Revelation 16:10-11).

By good seed is to be understood the children of the kingdom, who were joint-heirs with Christ of the kingdom of glory; and these at the last day shall be received up into the third heaven, "and shall shine forth

---

[4] "εἰς ζωὴν αἰώνιον." (Matt. 25:46).

as the sun in the kingdom of their Father," and that forevermore; for of his kingdom there shall be no end, (Matthew 13:38, 43).

This divine doctrine may be further illustrated and yet more strongly confirmed by these two Scriptural arguments:

1. First, at the great judicial proceedings of the whole world, when all mankind shall so "appear," (2 Corinthians 5:10) before the tribunal of Christ, as that the secrets of their hearts shall be laid open, they will be found either such as were ignorant and disobedient, and out of Christ, or such as were knowing, obedient, and interested in Christ.

Those who shall be found at that notable day of discovery, such as had no part in Christ, "such as knew not God, and as obeyed not the Gospel of our Lord Jesus Christ, shall be punished with everlasting destruction from the presence of the Lord, and from the glory of his power," (2 Thessalonians 1:7).

But those who are found at that great day of trial, such as were in Christ, "such as did know the only true God, and Jesus Christ whom he hath sent," (John 17:3, 6:40): and such as truly believed in Christ, and sincerely obeyed him shall be saved with "eternal salvation," (Hebrews 5:9).

Therefore, *all* mankind at the end of the world shall go into an everlasting condition, either of woe or rejoicing.

2. Secondly, either all mankind after the day of judgment shall go into an everlasting condition, either of happiness, or misery; or else some of mankind shall be turned into nothing: or else some of mankind shall go into some third place or state. Which is true?

Scripture does not teach that any of mankind shall be turned into "nothing," (Matthew 25:46); for the wicked of all mankind shall go into "everlasting punishment," therefore they shall have an everlasting being. Otherwise there would be a punishment inflicted, and none endured, which is a contradiction. And the righteous among mankind shall go into "life eternal," and, therefore, they shall subsist and live forever. So, none of mankind shall be annihilated, or consumed and turned into nothing.

Nor shall any of mankind go into any third place or state, because there is no place nor state to be found in the Word of God for any of mankind to go into, after this world is ended, besides "hell and heaven," besides the cursed condition of everlasting punishment, and the blessed state of life eternal (Matthew 7:13-14; Luke 16; Matthew 25:46). And how can any of mankind go into that which is not?

Therefore, we may certainly conclude, "That all mankind at the end of this world shall go into their bodies and souls into an everlasting condition either of glory or misery." The wicked shall go into an everlasting condition of pain and calamity, and the righteous shall go into an everlasting condition of rest and glory, and so all shall go into an eternal state, either of felicity or misery, after that time shall be no longer.

Here it might be shown that the doctrine of man's everlasting condition in the world to come, has been received for a truth ever since this world began. The holy patriarchs, Prophets, and Apostles, and the Old and New Testament saints believed it, and acknowledged it.[5] So did the ancient fathers after them, and the greatest part of Christians in all ages and parts of the world. And all the Reformed Churches now in Christendom confess it, and earnestly contend for this fundamental article of the universal faith of believers.

---

[5] Genesis 2:17, 3:15, 24; Hebrews 11: 4-5, 7-9, 11:26; Jude 14-15; Daniel 12:2; Matthew 25:46; 2 Thessalonians 3:8-10.

Chapter 2: Happiness or Misery

But I labor to be brief, and therefore instead of insisting upon the antiquity of this point, I shall refer you to the Scriptures and authors in the margin,[6] and to the last article of Athanasius' Creed, of the Nicene Creed, and of that ancient creed, commonly called the Apostle's Creed, whereby by which you may see with your own eyes that this is no new, but an ancient truth, which has been received in the church of God, in all ages of the world.

2. Secondly, this infallible doctrine may be proved, if further proof is needful, by human testimony, and as I may say with the Apostle, (Acts 17:28) by certain of our own poets; for, the wiser sort both of poets and philosophers were of this opinion, "That wicked people shall go after they depart hence, into a horrible place called *Tartarus*, where they shall be eternally tormented. And that good men shall go after their departure out of this life, into a pleasant place, called *Eliziam*, where they shall live happily forever."[7] Their opinion clearly shows that they had some imperfect notions of man's future eternity, either in torment or happiness.

---

[6] Daille of the use of the fathers; his preface and p. 184 & *Corpus Confes.*

[7] See P. Mornay of the truths of the Christian religion; ch.15, 19. V. Grot. l.1 c.21, 22, 63 l.4 c.12.

Again, those who write about the world tell us that the people of every nation in the world are of some religion,[8] and those who are of any religion hold that there is a life after this life, where it shall go well with the good, and ill with the bad of mankind forever; why else are they religious?[9]

It is without a doubt, that it must necessarily be a manifest truth, that appears to be so, not only by the light of the holy Scriptures, but also by the light of nature, and the common opinion (almost) of all people in the world. No, by the common practice of the devil himself, "Who as a roaring lion walketh about seeking whom he may devour," (1 Peter 5:8) endeavoring by his temptations, apparitions, possessions, and wiles with deluded sinners, to disprove as many of mankind of eternal salvation as he possibly can, and to bring them at last to everlasting damnation, from which, *good Lord deliver us.*

---

[8] Munster, *Ortelius Heylyn.* See P. Mornay; c.1 p. 9.
[9] *Koran,* Mahom. c.14 p. 160; c.20 p. 198.

Chapter 3:
Misery of the Wicked

Describing the misery of that everlasting condition of woe and punishment that the wicked shall go into at the end of the world.

Having so far proved the doctrine of man's future eternity, I shall, in the next place, explain it. First of all, I shall mournfully look downward, toward the miserable eternity of such as shall be damned, and show you (so far as I know it by Scripture's revelation) the misery of their everlasting punishment, which is the *punishment of punishments*, and what that chiefly consists, namely in these three particulars. 1) In their punishment of loss, 2) In their pain of sense, and 3) In the everlastingness of both of these kinds of punishment.

1. First the misery of that everlasting cursed and damned condition that the wicked shall go into at the end of this world, consists in their punishment of loss, and that in these four respects:

1]. They shall be punished with the loss of the comfortable and beatific presence of God the Father,

Son, and Holy Spirit. "They shall depart and go away from the Lord," in such a sort as that they shall never have any favor, nor any refreshing from the presence of the ever blessed and glorious Trinity.

God being the chief good,[1] and the greatest felicity, and his lovingkindness being better than life, therefore to be punished with the loss of his favor will be as it were the everlasting death of the damned, and their greatest loss, and saddest misery.

2]. They shall be punished with the loss of heaven, that place of celestial rest and blessedness, where God is said to dwell, where Christ has ascended, and where the Lord will manifest himself to his people to their everlasting comfort and happiness. "There shall be weeping and gnashing of teeth (our Savior says) when ye shall see Abraham, and Isaac, and Jacob, and all the Prophets in the kingdom of God, and you yourselves thrust out," (Luke 13:28).

3]. They shall be punished with the loss of the blessed communion of all the holy angels in heaven; for seeing they shall be punished with the loss of the favorable presence of God, and with the loss of heaven, it follows that they shall be punished with the loss of the

---

[1] Psalm 113:68; Matthew 19:17; Psalm 36:9; Psalm 63:3.

Chapter 3: Misery of the Wicked

joyful fellowship of all the holy angels, "who do always behold the face of God in heaven," (Matthew 18:10).

4]. They shall be punished with the loss of the comfortable company of all the saints in heaven, and of all their glorious perfections, and heavenly privileges; for since they shall depart from the Lord,[2] and shall be shut out of heaven, and cast into hell, where they shall forever remain unpardoned and unsanctified, retaining their vile hearts and sinful natures. Therefore, it necessarily follows that they shall be deprived of the happy society of all the saints, and of all those celestial perfections and blessed privileges that they shall enjoy when they shall be ever with the Lord in the kingdom of heaven, (Luke 16:22-27).

We think their loss to be very great, who are punished with the loss of the temporal good things of this life; but alas! What is that to the loss of the eternal good things of the life to come?

A godly gentleman observing the gallant accommodations of a pious noble man,[3] took occasion to speak to him after this Christian manner, "My Lord, (he said) you had need make sure of heaven, or else when

---

[2] Luke 13:25,27-28; John 8:24
[3] This is related by Mr. Edmund Calamy in his sermon on Hebrews 11:13.

you die, you will be a great loser;" it infinitely concerns both great and small, to make sure work about their salvation, otherwise when they die they will be *great losers*, for they will lose not only their comforts on earth, but also the joys of heaven, and that without all hope of recovery, (Luke 16:23-24).

2. Secondly, the misery of that woeful and cursed condition, called the "damnation of hell," (Matthew 23:33) that the wicked shall go into, after the day of judgment, consists in their pain of sense, or in that sensible pain that they shall be punished withal in hell, that terrible place of torment, and that in various particulars, is worthy of our most serious consideration.

1]. They shall be punished universally with a sensible pain, all over; as, in their bodies, and in all its parts, and in their souls, and in all its faculties. "Those shall go away into everlasting punishment;" it is spoken of the wicked, after they were condemned to go in their bodies and souls into "Everlasting fire, prepared for the devil and his angels," (Matthew 25:41, 46).

2]. They shall be punished extremely, with a grievous sensible torment in their whole man; for, "They shall go into [4] hell into the fire that never shall be

---

[4] Psalm 9:17.

quenched,[5] and into the lake that burns with fire and brimstone," (Mark 9:4,6, Revelation 21:8).

Though fire and brimstone are terrible, yet the thing thereby signified is more terrible; indeed, the largest and most capacious heart alive cannot conceive how extreme their pain and misery will be, upon whom the "total wrath of God shall abide forever," (John 3:36, Revelation 14:10).

If Cain, if Judas, if Spira, and others were so grievously tormented with despair and horror of conscience, when the terrors of God were on them. And if the wrath of God on Christ for a while, caused his soul to be exceedingly heavy, and made his body sweat as it were "great drops of blood," (Luke 22:44), how extreme will the infinite fierce wrath of God torment the damned in hell, when it shall abide on them for all eternity?

3]. They shall be punished continually, without having any ease, intermission, or freedom from pain throughout the infinite space of eternity. How can it be otherwise, since they shall be cast into the "Bottomless pit of hell, where their worm dieth not, and the fire is not

---

[5] Psalm 9:17.

quenched; where they have no rest day nor night,"[6] but are tormented continually, (Revelation 14:10-11).

I have sometimes thought in my sickness, "What if the Lord should always afflict me with such a pain as this, and should continue me to endure it to all eternity, how miserable then would my life be? And yet, (says a learned author, after a long sickness) [7] "What is a sickbed to hell? What is a fever to those everlasting burnings? Where the fits never end, the fire never goeth out, the worm never dieth," (Mark 9:44).

4]. They shall be punished remedilessly, without ever having any remedy, or any help, or hope of remedy. The author to the Hebrews tells us, "That if we sin willfully, after we have received the knowledge of the truth, there remaineth no more sacrifice for sins, but a certain fearful looking for of judgment, and fiery indignation, which shall devour the adversaries," (Hebrews 10:26-27).

The sacrifice of Christ is the only[8] true sacrifice, if that is quite rejected, it can be no more reiterated, neither can there be any other found elsewhere, and so

---

[6] Revelation 20:2-3; Mark 9:43.
[7] Dr. Arrowsmith's *Armilla Catechit.*, republished by Puritan Publications in updated language.
[8] Deodat. *Annot.*

nothing but remediless misery is to be expected; those who shall finally refuse Jesus Christ, our ever dear Redeemer, shall be condemned to hell without all possibility of being redeemed out of it, and without all hope of having any comfort in it.[9] And so, they will be left to utter desperation, without either help or hope of remedy; but here is not all, *for:*

3. Thirdly, the misery of that deplorable punishment, and fullness of all cursedness, called, "The second death," (Revelation 25:8) which impenitent unbelievers and ill-believers must endure in hell, at the end of the world, consists in its everlastingness. Their punishment of loss, and pain of sense, will last throughout all eternity.

Hearken what the Scripture says about the miserable eternity of such as shall be damned, "They shall go away into everlasting punishment; they shall suffer the vengeance of eternal fire; the blackness of darkness is reserved for them forever; they shall be tormented forever and ever," (Matthew 25:46; Jude v. 7, 13; Revelation 20:10).

---

[9] Psalm 49:7-8. Luke 16:24-26.

O! these words, "Everlasting sting, eternal, ever, ever and everlasting,"[10] how plainly and fully do they prove the everlastingness, and perpetuity of the punishment of the damned in hell? After they have been punished with the loss of the happiness of heaven, and with the sense of the horror of hell, as many years as there are grass piles on the earth, as there are drops of water in the sea, as there are sands by the seashore, as there are motes in the sun, as there have been leaves on all the trees that ever grew, and as there have been hairs upon the heads of all mankind from the first until the last born. I say, after they have been punished so many years, no, more, after they have been punished so many millions of years as it is possible for the mind of man to conceive, their most fearful punishment will be no nearer an end, for it will ever last and never end, never, never.

Their souls are immortal already,[11] and their bodies shall be raised everlasting: the judgment that shall be passed on them is eternal, hell, that place of torment, they shall be turned into, continues forever. Their worm of conscience is ever-living, and the wrath

---

[10] Matthew 25:46.
[11] Ecclesiastes 12:7; Daniel 12:2; Hebrews 6:2; 2 Peter 2:17; Mark 9:45; John 3:35.

Chapter 3: Misery of the Wicked

of God which shall abide on them is everlasting; therefore, their punishment shall be everlasting, everlasting.

Though we may look forward, and so forward considering their miserable eternity, yet we shall never see the end of it, and they will never find an end of it; for, after it is once begun, it is like a circle that has no end at all, or like that prison, that whosoever were cast into it, could never get out again.[12]

In all the miseries mankind meets with in this world, they have this poor comfort, they hope their misery will have an end. But the wicked in hell can have no such hope, and therefore, no such comfort; for, they will know after Christ has condemned them to go into everlasting fire, that their punishment will be everlasting and endless.

If any say to me, "What is the eternity of the damned in hell?" My reply is this, it is the everlastingness of their hellish pain and misery, by which it will last forever, and never end, *never, never.*

O! all you careless sinners! See here in this miserable *eternity, eternity, eternity,* the great and abominable evil of sin, and the sad fruit of it. See here,

---

[12] The Persian's prison, called *Lethe Daexel.*

what that wrath to come is, you ought to flee from, and how much it concerns you to fear God, who can cast both soul and body into hell.[13] See here, where the broad way of affected ignorance, unbelief, and wickedness will end, even within the wide gate of the dreadful prison of hell, from once there is no return. Behold here, what your sins will bring you to at last, unless you truly repent of them, and apply Christ by faith for pardon of them, and power against them.

And do not flatter yourselves in hope of a tolerable hell, as thinking that if you are damned, that you may endure the torments of hell as well as others. For *verily, verily,* no finite heart can conceive how great the pain and misery of the damned will be, who shall be punished by an infinite God, for an infinite space of eternity. One says well, "We can go no further in comprehending that which is incomprehensible, than to know it to be incomprehensible."[14]

It is not for nothing "that God hath ordained Tophet of old," (Isaiah 30:33; Matthew 5:22, 25:41, 46; Mark 5:43-44, 46) and that Christ has so often threatened hell and everlasting punishment against

---

[13] Matthew 10:18; Luke 12:5.
[14] Mr. Dent's *The Plain Man's Pathway to Heaven.*

Chapter 3: Misery of the Wicked

impenitent and unbelieving sinners. For, for as sure as the promises of heaven and life eternal are true, so sure are the threatenings of hell and everlasting punishment are true, and they shall be fulfilled in God's appointed time and way, (Matthew 5:18, 25:46).

Though reprobate sinners are but finite creatures, and sinned but for a time, yet because they sinned against an infinitely good God, and against the everlasting Gospel of Jesus Christ, the eternal Son of God, and never repented of their sins, but would have sinned eternally if they had lived eternally,[15] therefore the offense is infinite, and it will be just with God to punish them with an everlasting punishment, and so with an infinite punishment in respect of duration, (Romans 3:8, 6:23).

Although all the damned shall be everlastingly punished with the loss of the happiness of heaven, and with the sense of the misery of hell, yet by how much any of them have been greater sinners than others of them, by so much their degrees of punishment will be the greater,[16] according to the opinion of most expositors on

---

[15] Aquinas, Q.87. art.5 and Suppl. Par. 3 q.99 art.1.
[16] V. Gerard. *de inferno*.

these texts of Scripture: Matthew 11:22-23, 23:14; Luke 12:47-48.

If the worm in hell that dies not, and the fire that is not quenched are material, as some learned writers suppose they are,[17] then the damned in hell will be grievously and everlastingly tormented with them. And if they are metaphorical, as it is most likely they are, according to the judgment of several modern divines,[18] than the conscience of the damned sinners will be like a worm that dies not, and the wrath of God abiding on them, will be like the fire that is not quenched, tormenting them universally, eternally.

But what need is there to curiously inquire, or boldly to determine about such niceties as these? It is enough to know that the pains and torments of hell to the wicked will be both eternal and incomprehensible, (Deuteronomy 29:29).

Oh reader! If we, who know but in part, "The doctrine of the everlasting punishment of such as shall be damned," do apprehend their misery to be so exceedingly grievous. How extremely miserable will

---

[17] Aug. *de civ. Dei*, l. 21 c. 9-10. Lombard, l. 4 Dist. 44 Suppl. 3 par. Qu. 97, art. 5.
[18] Calvin in Isaiah 30:33; Tilenus Syntag. p. 2 d. 47 Gerard *de inferno*.

Chapter 3: Misery of the Wicked

they find their punishment to be, when they shall fully know it, by woeful experience?

As that youth,[19] who was chosen by a certain king who had no issue, to be heir to the crown, in case he proved fit for government, otherwise to be a galley-slave, came to know by sad experience how great his punishment was for his negligence and misdemeanor, when (being found on trial unfit for a kingly throne) instead of being crowned king, he was made a galley-slave. Even so, the wicked will come to know by woeful experience, how great their punishment shall be, for their willful ignorance and final disobedience, when instead of being preferred to heaven, to be ever with the Lord, and with his holy angels and saints, they shall be condemned to go into hellfire, "prepared for the devil and his angels;" their infernal tormenting; and tormented companions, (Matthew 25:34, 41).

O! what cause have we (who have deserved to be everlastingly damned) have delivered "us from this wrath to come, through Jesus Christ," (1 Thessalonians 1:10; cf. 1 Corinthians 15:57), to "wish out" of our zeal to his glory, that all our thoughts, words, and works, may either honor Christ, or dishonor ourselves.

---

[19] Bellarm. in *Concione de crucia tibus Gehenna*.

Chapter 4:
Glory for the Righteous

Explaining the happiness of that eternal state of glory and rest, that the righteous shall go into at the last day.

I have already cast my eyes downward toward the miserable eternity of such as shall be damned, and described the horror of it to you, therefore, I shall next of all joyfully look upward towards the blessed eternity of such as shall be saved, and show you (so far as I have attained to see it by Scripture's light) in what the happiness of their eternal life, which is the life of lives, principally consists. In other words, in these three things: 1) In their being like Christ, 2) In their enjoyment of God in Christ, and 3) In the eternity of both these heavenly privileges.

1. First, the happiness of that eternal blessed and glorious state, that the righteous shall go into on the last day, consists in their being made like Christ. The Apostle John says, "That when Christ shall appear, we shall be like him." As Christ is holy and glorious in soul and body, so his people at his appearing shall be holy and glorious in their souls and bodies, and so they shall be

"like their Savior in holiness and glory." They will not be this way in equality, but in resemblance,[1] and so with a difference of degrees between head and members, (1 John 3:2).

The souls of all those who died in Christ before his second coming, were immediately after the death of their bodies, and at a particular judgment, acquitted and made perfect in holiness and glory,[2] like the glorified soul of their Savior. And when their bodies shall be raised again at the last day, "They shall be fashioned like to his glorious body, and so they shall awake in his likeness," (Psalm 17:15; Philippians 3:21).

The people of Christ also, who shall be found alive at his appearing, "shall be like him." Indeed, all of God's saints shall be conformable to their blessed Savior in perfect purity and glory,[3] and so they shall be fully freed in their whole man from all sin, both original and actual, and from all sorts of sorrows, miseries and sufferings which are external, internal and eternal. But also, they shall be completely endowed in their bodies and souls with such pure and heavenly qualities as the blessed manhood of Christ is now glorified with. As, in

---

[1] *Similes non paves;* Beza *ep.* 1 John 3:2.
[2] Hebrews 12:23.
[3] 1 Corinthians 15:49.

their bodies, with "immortality, spirituality, power, and glory," (1 Corinthians 15:42-44, 53), and in their souls with "perfect light of understanding."[4] By this they shall know even as they are known, and with "perfect freedom of will," by which they shall be exactly conformable to the heavenly will of God. And, again, with "perfect order and elevation of affection," by which they shall perfectly love and praise the Lord their God, and perpetually delight themselves in him. And, so being glorified in their bodies and souls, they will be fitted for that state of glory and eternal life that they shall inherit from that time forth, and forever, (Matthew 25:46, 1 Peter 5:4).

"Thus, when Christ who is their life shall appear, then shall they also appear with him in glory," (Colossians 3:4). They will be clothed with the white robes of his "everlasting righteousness and splendor: not having spot or wrinkle, or any such thing;" and so Christ will present them "holy and glorious"[5] in the kingdom of heaven, where he will uphold them in perfect purity and glory "world without end," insomuch as that *he* will be

---

[4] Psalm 36:9; 1 Corinthians 13:12; Matthew 6:10; Revelation 19:1.
[5] Isaiah 60:21; Ephesians 5:27; Colossians 1:22.

everlastingly "glorified and admired in them," (2 Thessalonians 1:10; Hebrews 13:8; Revelation 21:23).

Though we, poor as we are, do not know as yet how glorious our Savior is in heaven at this time, nor consequently how glorious his people shall be when they shall be like him, yet we may guess at the glory of Christ in heaven, by the glory of his transfiguration on earth.[6] We may safely conclude that the saints will be satisfied when they shall perfectly bear their Savior's celestial image in the kingdom of heaven, and that then they will have cause to say, as Peter did on the mountain, "It is good for us to be here," (Matthew 17:4).

If the man who had been long sick, joyed to think that in the grace he should be free from pain and sickness, how may the children of God, who have been long sick of sinning, and subject to suffering all their life long, rejoice, to think that in heaven, when they "shall be like Christ," will be beyond all possibility of sinning and suffering, (1 Corinthians 15:54-57, Revelation 21:4).

2. Secondly, the happiness of that joyful and blessed life, called everlasting life, that the saints shall inherit in their bodies and souls after the day of judgment, consists in their enjoyment of God in Christ,

---

[6] Matthew 17:2.

in the "everlasting habitations" of heaven; which is the principal part of the happiness of their eternal life, and as it were, the highest pitch of their heavenly contentment and joy.

All the elect people of God, by whatsoever names and religions they were called, and distinguished here on earth, they shall in heaven have all communion one with another, fellowship with the holy angels, and a full fruition of that ever-blessed Godhead in Trinity of persons. This is had in three respects, which I shall the rather express in Scriptural language for the help of our weak understanding in it.

1. They shall enjoy God in Christ, in being present with him in the same high heaven, and ever-blessed eternity, where he enjoys himself, and where his glorious angels and the blessed souls of his people enjoy him. "For thus saith the high and lofty One that inhabiteth eternity, whose name is Holy; I dwell in the high and holy place, with him also that is of a contrite and humble spirit, to revive the spirit of the humble, and to revive the heart of the contrite ones," (Isa. 57:15).

Christ has promised his people, "that he will receive them to himself; that where he is, there they may be also," (John 14:3); and therefore, they shall be there in his appointed time.

Again, the Apostle Paul plainly tells us, "that we shall be ever with the Lord," (1 Thessalonians 4:17). And so we shall partake of that fulness of joy that is in his presence, and of those pleasures which are at his right hand forevermore, (Psalm 16:11).

This is that which the saints here on earth do so earnestly and ardently desire, as that their souls are restless and unsatisfied until they come to the full fruition of God in the highest heaven, which he has prepared for their everlasting home and entertainment in the world to come.[7]

2. They shall enjoy God in seeing him as he is; For, then says Saint Paul, "we shall see face to face," and "know even as we are known," (1 Corinthians 13:12).[8]

Again, the Apostle John says that we "shall see the Lord as he is;" and so we shall enjoy him by our immediate and blessed vision of him, (1 John 3:2).

All the saints shall behold the glory of their blessed Savior in his heavenly kingdom with the eyes of

---

[7] 2 Corinthians 5:2, 8; Philippians 1:23. *Secisti nos; & canqui enum est Cor,* and Augustine. *Conf.* lib.1 c.1.
[8] Sicut Angelivident; ita & nos visuri sumus. Augustine *de Civ. dei*, lib.21 c.29.

their glorified bodies;[9] and they shall see the blessed deity in three glorious persons, with the eyes of their understanding fully enlightened with the light of glory.[10] They shall all know the Lord apprehensively in all his admirable excellencies and perfections, and they shall see him whom their soul loves as it were "face to face," clearly and perfectly, and so they shall have a full satisfactory knowledge of God, who is the first *Truth*, and of all other truths which may conduce to their complete happiness.

Zwingerus was so fully persuaded of this, as that he said at the point of death, "I am glad that the time is now come when the Lord will show himself unto me face to face."[11]

3. They shall enjoy God in Christ, in being perfectly one with the Father and Him, as they are one, after such a real manner, as that they shall never be parted from him, but shall be indissolubly joined to him, to their unspeakable comfort and happiness.

Jesus Christ, who cannot but be heard, has prayed both for the beginning and the accomplishment of this blessed union. His prayer is, "That all his people

---

[9] Job 19:25-26; John 17:24.
[10] Isaiah 60:19-20; Matthew 5:8; Revelation 22:4-5.
[11] Melch. *Adam. vit. Germ.* p. 416.

Chapter 4: Glory for the Righteous

may be one with the Father and Him, as they are one," (John 17:21-23). They cannot therefore but be partakers of this blissful oneness with the blessed Trinity; and being partakers of it, they will enjoy God by their happy conjunction, and immediate communion with him.

All believers through the Holy Spirit, are now inseparably united to the glorious person of the Son of God, as members to their Head, and by Christ they are united to God the Father, the Fountain of grace and glory, by which they are now made partakers of the divine light and life of grace, (2 Peter 1:4).[12]

And this spiritual and mystical union begun here, shall be perfected forever hereafter, by which they shall partake of the everlasting light and life of glory immediately from the Lord of glory, in such a heavenly, all-satisfying sort, as that they shall be as fully happy as they possibly can wish or desire to be.[13]

As all the elect shall be beatifically united to God in Christ, so they shall be perfectly united one to another in judgment, will, and affection;[14] however, as much as they differed on earth, they shall all agree in heaven, in one scope and act of giving glory and praise to God, and

---

[12] Ephesians 2:22, 5:30, 32.
[13] Isaiah 60:19; Revelation 21:23.
[14] John 17:21-22; Hebrews 10:22-23; Revelation 7:9-12.

in one perpetual adoration, and fruition of one infinite deity in Trinity of persons; and so they will be mutually happy in God, in themselves, and in each other.

Although it is the soul which enjoys God, or that partakes of the good which is in God;[15] yet the body also shall have a share in the happiness of the soul's enjoyment of God in the kingdom of glory, (1 Thessalonians 4:16-17).

Since God is an infinite, self-existing Spirit, from eternity, in eternity, to eternity,[16] and is his own happiness and the author and object of all happiness, therefore the full enjoyment of God "blessed forever," who is self-sufficient" in his being, and "all-sufficient" in his communications, will be a satisfying felicity, and as high an happiness as either saints or angels can desire to enjoy, (Psalm 73:25-26).

I could not be affectionately taken with the judgment of a pious writer about this particular; "Inquire (he says) of such as are yet militant upon earth, in which their happiness consists, the answer will be, "In their having fellowship with the Father, and with his Son, Jesus Christ;" let those who are triumphant be

---

[15] Manchester *contemplemort & immort.*
[16] Exodus 3:14; Psalm 50:1; Romans 1:25; Ephesians 1:3.

asked, What it is that renders their heaven so glorious; their glory so incomprehensible, you shall have no other account but this, it is because they have now attained a complete fruition of that all-sufficient, all-satisfying, ever-blessed, and ever-blessing object-God in Christ."[17]

It is the doctrinal observation of a worthy preacher, [18] "That God alone is more desirable than anything, than all things in heaven and earth;" and no wonder if we consider, "That the Lord is such a depth of divine perfections, as that he professes in one only perfection, and excellency of all perfections, in so excellent sort, as that none is able to comprehend it but himself, therefore the everlasting enjoyment of him can be no other than perfect blessedness."

We may piously think according to the Scriptures, that when the saints shall partake of this heavenly fruition of God in Christ, they will have such a full sense and real experience of the everlasting love of God unto them, as that they will be forever [19]affected with it, and constrained by it, perfectly to love the Lord their God, perpetually to rejoice in him, and everlastingly to laud him and praise him for their blessed

---

[17] Dr. Arrowsmith *Armilla Chatechet.*
[18] Dr. Annesley's sermon upon Psalm 73:25.
[19] Song of Solomon 5:8; 2 Corinthians 5:14.

enjoyment of him; and so their love to God, joy in him, and thankfulness to him shall never cease, because it is a part of that heavenly happiness which will redound from their beatific fruition of God in Christ.[20]

"A day in thy courts (sacred King David says to God) is better than a thousand; I had rather be a doorkeeper in the house of my God, than to dwell in the tents of wickedness," (Psalm 84:20). If the enjoyment of God in his ordinances is so unspeakably sweet and delightful, how incomprehensibly comfortable and complacent will the saint's perfect fruition of God in heaven be!

I do not know how to express it, let your souls think of it; but there is more yet, *for:*

3. Thirdly, the perfect blessedness of that happy condition of heavenly rest and glory, called an eternal weight of glory, that penitent and pious believers shall go into at the last day; consists in the eternity of it, their glorious conformity unto Christ, and then blessed enjoyment of God in Christ, will never end, nor ever alter, but will continue to be the same forever.

Hear what sacred writ says concerning the saint's future eternity, "They shall go into life eternal,

---

[20] 1 Corinthians 13:8,13; Psalm 16:11; Revelation 5:11-12.

they shall have everlasting life, they shall ever live, and never die; they shall be ever with the Lord, and shall reign with him forever and ever in the kingdom of glory, where they shall wear an incorruptible crown of life and glory, and where they shall possess an eternal inheritance, incorruptible, and undefiled, and that fades not away," (1 Peter 1:4).[21]

How clearly and fully do these words, "Eternal, everlasting, forever, ever, and ever," prove that the blessed life or happy condition of, that the righteous shall go into at the last day, will never end, but ever continue, forever, ever, and ever?

After the saints in heaven have been happy in their glorious conformity unto Christ, and in their blessed enjoyment of God in Christ, as many years as there are stars in the heavens, as there have been drops of water rained down from heaven since the beginning of the world, as there have been things thought upon, words spoken, and actions done by all mankind since the day that God created man; and as there have been letters written and printed, since letters, writing, and printing were found out in the world; when they have

---

[21] Matthew 25:45; John 3:16; 6:51; 11:26; 1 Thessalonians 4:17; Revelation 22:5; 1 Corinthians 9:25; James 1:15; 1 Peter 5:4; Hebrews 9:15.

lived with the Lord in heavenly, glory and happiness so many years, no, so many thousands of years, [22] this blessed life will be no nearer an end, for it will last forever, and never end, "Because I live (Christ says to his disciples) ye shall live also," (John 14:19; Revelation 1:18). As Christ, who is the head of his Church, lives forevermore, so his people who are his members shall live forevermore; and in this respect he will satisfy them with long life, even with everlasting life, which had indeed a beginning, but shall never have an end, (Psalm 91:16; John 10:28).

Their souls are immortal by creation,[23] and their bodies shall be immortal at their resurrection; the heaven of heavens, which they shall inhabit, is eternal. Their God, whom they shall enjoy, is everlasting, their blessed Head and Savior, in whom they shall enjoy the Lord, is ever-living. Therefore, their blessed life shall be everlasting, forever and ever, yes, *everlasting*.

What more can I say? After the inheritors of the kingdom of heaven have lived in celestial glory and felicity, as many millions of years as all mankind could ever number, they will be as far off from the end of their

---

[22] Psalm 90:4.
[23] Matthew 10:28; 1 Corinthians 15:53; 2 Corinthians 5:1; Genesis 21:33; Hebrews 7:25.

everlasting blessedness as they were at the beginning of it; for their blessed and eternal eternity (after they are once entered into it) is like a ring, that has no end at all, and it shall be as an immortal ring, which they shall eternally wear, in remembrance of the Lord's everlasting love unto them.

All our earthly enjoyments are damped, and made less comfortable to us, because they are but temporal,[24] for a while, we may leave them, or they may leave us, today before tomorrow. But the heavenly enjoyments of the saints in glory, are heightened and made more happy and joyful, because they are eternal, and will be altogether the same, forever and ever, (1 Thessalonians 4:17; Hebrews 13:8).

If any now ask me, what is the saint's eternity in heaven, my answer is this; It is the infinite length of their blessed life, and heavenly happiness, by which it will never end, but ever continue, forever, ever, and ever.

O! all you blessed and *thrice* happy saints, see here this blessed *eternity, eternity, eternity,* what the Lord has prepared for those that wait on him. See here, where the narrow way of humility, faith, and piety will end, even within the strait gate of the great city of

---

[24] 2 Corinthians 4:18; Proverbs 23:5; Luke 12:20.

heaven, where are joys inconceivable, and pleasures forevermore. Behold here, how those that sow in tears, shall reap in joy, and how the Lord will in mercy reward those with the enjoyment of himself, who diligently seek him, (Hebrews 11:6).

And rejoice (you happy heirs of heaven) rejoice in the hope and expectation of this heavenly glory and happiness to come, [25] and comfort one another with these things, and let the joy and recompense of reward which has been set before you, move you to go on unweariedly in the ways of God, "always abounding in the work of the Lord, forasmuch as ye know that your labor is not in vain in the Lord," (1 Corinthians 15:58; Hebrews 12:2).

Though all the saints shall be members and fellow-citizens of the heavenly Jerusalem, and shall be fully and everlastingly happy in their holy and glorious conformity to Christ, and in their blessed enjoyment of God in Christ, yet, it is probable, by how much any of them (through the grace of Christ) have glorified God on earth, more than others of them, by so much their degrees of glory in heaven will be the greater, according to the judgment of most divines upon these places of

---

[25] Romans 5:3; 1 Thessalonians 4:18.

Chapter 4: Glory for the Righteous

Scripture: Daniel 12:3; Matthew 10:41-42, 19:28; 1 Corinthians 3:8; 2 Corinthians 4:17; 2 Corinthians 9:6.[26]

It is the general opinion of godly learned men, that the saints in heaven will perfectly and personally know one another, to the mutual comfort one of another; this is usually proved by arguments taken from these texts of Scripture: Matthew 17:1-4, 8:11; Luke 16:23; 1 Corinthians 13:12.

After the resurrection the saints "will neither marry, nor be given in marriage, but shall be as the angels of God in heaven," (Matthew 22:30). And their bodies being spiritual in quality, they shall be freed from the necessities and imperfections of the animal life, and upheld immediately by the Almighty power of God, without the use of food and raiment, and all other means that are requisite to the preservation of the life that now is, (1 Corinthians 15:28).

When all the saints shall be like Christ, and shall be brought to the blissful fruition of God in Christ, in those eternal mansions of heaven assigned for them, then prophesying, hearing, and praying, and all duties, graces, and actions that were used as means to that blessed end,

---

[26] Augustine *de Civ dei*, lib. 22 c. 30; Aqinas. *suppl.* 3 par. qu. 96; art. 11. Calvin, *Inst.* lib. 3 c. 25 s. 10. Bucan. *Inst.* loc. 39 p. 4, 6.

shall cease, and then they shall have that everlasting rest that now remains for them,[27] which is the endless rest of rests; and so they shall keep that everlasting Sabbath, which is the Sabbath of Sabbaths; and the eternal God himself (who is goodness and perfection wholly incomprehensible) shall be with them, and will be their God, their exceeding great reward, their portion, their heaven, their life eternal, their happiness, and "their all in all," (1 Corinthians 15:28; Revelation 21:3). With whom they will be fully satisfied, and in whom they will comfortably acquiesce, and contentedly rest to all eternity; yea, "the Lord their God will rejoice over them with joy, and will rest in his love unto them," (Zephaniah 3:17).

O sirs! If the blessedness of the life to come is but revealed in part, and if we who know but part of that part of it, which is revealed, and that through a glass darkly, conceive the glory and bliss of it, to be unspeakably great. How inconceivably glorious and blessed will the saints in heaven find it to be, when they shall fully know it by comfortable experience?

In sum, the happiness of heaven and of the blessed life to come called by divines, "the state of

---

[27] 1 Corinthians 13:8; Hebrews 4:9.

glorification," is such as that it will please and satisfy all, who shall have a part in it, and it is infinitely greater and better than can be uttered or conceived, therefore let us humbly leave the rest of the felicity of it, to the future experience of such as shall enjoy it, as we may hope, we shall within a short time, if our hearts are right in the sight of God.[28]

It is reported of the Duke of Bouillon and his army, that when they went to Jerusalem, as soon as they saw the high turrets, they shouted for joy, "crying out Jerusalem, Jerusalem;" what cause have we poor pilgrims and strangers on the earth, who are travelling towards the celestial Jerusalem, our heavenly country, to rejoice with joy unspeakable, as soon as we see by faith any glimpse of the exceeding glory and happiness of it, saying with a joyful noise to God, "Hallelujah, Hallelujah, blessed and forever blessed be the Lord," "that we know that if our earthly house of this tabernacle were dissolved, we have a building of God, an house not made with hands, eternal in the heavens," (2 Corinthians 5:1); A house? Yea, "a palace of heavenly state and magnificence; neither is it less than a kingdom that abides there for us: a kingdom so much above these

---

[28] 1 Corinthians 2:9; 2 Corinthians 12:4.

worldly monarchies, as heaven is above this clod of earth."

Chapter 5:
Bodies and Souls

Renders the principal reasons why all mankind after the day of judgment shall go in their bodies and souls into an everlasting condition, either of happiness or misery.

The great and important truth of man's eternal state to come, having been both proved and explained, I shall now give you its reasons, which are principally these two:

1. First, the elect of God among all mankind, who were interested in Christ, shall go in their bodies and souls, after they have received their joyful sentence of absolution, into an everlasting condition of happiness, for the everlasting glorifying of the mercy of God, (Romans 9:23).

Jesus Christ shall say to his elect people in the sight and hearing of all the world, "Come ye blessed of my Father, inherit the kingdom prepared for you from the foundation of the world," and afterward he shall bring them triumphantly into the possession of the everlasting kingdom of glory. Then, and from that time forth, and forever, it will be fully known that God is essentially merciful, and that his mercy toward those whom he has chosen in Christ to life eternal, is infinite, everlasting, and immutable, to the everlasting glory and honor of the mercy of the Lord, and to the perpetual praise of the glory of his grace, (Romans 9:23; Ephesians 1:5-6).[1]

As now the best of saints do but see the saving mercy of God towards them through a glass darkly, and do but weakly believe it, so they very imperfectly praise him for it. But when they shall perfectly know at the day of their complete redemption, that it was the mercy of God, and nothing but his tender mercy, and free grace in Christ towards them that elected them,[2] that created them, that redeemed them, that called them, that justified them, that sanctified them, and that has completely saved them, and for all this great end, that they might forever magnify him for it,[3] then, they will perfectly praise the Lord, and give him the glory due to his name, for this gracious and golden chain of mercy that reaches from their everlasting predestination, to

---

[1] Exodus 34:6-7; Psalm 103:17.
[2] Ephesians 1:3; Romans 8:29.
[3] *Finis vita eterna principatis est dei glorificatio.* Gerrard. *de vita aterna.*

their everlasting glorification, (Ephesians 1:3-6; Revelation 4:8-12).

As the saved in heaven will know by joyful experience the great things the Lord has done for them, and that it is eternal love to them in Christ that has delivered them from the nethermost hell, and that has brought them to the highest heaven, so they will affectionately praise him for it. They will delight to give glory to the Lord their God, who has brought them to his incomprehensible bliss and glory, through the communication of his grace and glory to them.

And as they will perfectly apprehend that the favor that God bears to them in Christ, shall endure forever and ever, so they will glorify him for it, forever and ever. They will sing without ceasing the high praises of God; not as the monks at Constantinople, who sung day and night divine praises to God, only one company after another. But *all* the elect angels and saints in heaven will unanimously and perpetually praise the everlasting God, Father, Son, and Holy Spirit, for the infinite felicity they shall enjoy together in his beatific presence, (Psalm 84:4; Revelation 7:10-12).

2. Secondly, all the reprobate of mankind, who had no part in Christ, shall go in their bodies and souls

immediately after the doleful sentence of condemnation has been pronounced against them, into an everlasting condition of misery, for the everlasting glorifying of the justice of God, (Romans 9:22).

When Jesus Christ shall say to the reprobate, in the presence of his elect angels and saints, "Depart from me ye cursed into everlasting fire, prepared for the devil and his angels," and when he shall at that instant cast them into hell, to be everlastingly punished; then, and ever after, it will be absolutely known that God is essentially just, and that his justice is infinite, eternal, and unchangeable, to the everlasting glory and honor of the justice of God, and to the eternal praise of his unalterable purpose to punish final impenitent and unbelieving sinners, according to the desert of their sins, (Romans 9:22; 2 Thessalonians 1:7-8).

The wicked in the world will not now believe the justice, anger, and displeasure of God, against sin and impenitent sinners, nor will they glorify it,[4] when it is executed on secured sinners, others in temporal or spiritual judgments. "But when the great day of the Lord's wrath is come,"[5] then they shall feel it by woeful

---

[4] Isaiah 26:10-11.
[5] *Ira Dei est infernus diaboli; & omnium damnatorum.* Luther.

experience, and shall be forced to know and acknowledge the Lord to be just and their damnation to be just, to the eternal praise and glory of the sovereign justice and wrath of God against final unconverted sinners, (Romans 3:8, Revelation 6:17).

It is the opinion of various of our English divines, that God intends "the glorifying of the two great attributes of his mercy and justice,"[6] most eminently at the day of judgment, and in the world to come. And surely the vessels of mercy and the vessels of wrath will find it so at the last day, and from that time forth to all eternity, (Job 21:29-31; 1 Peter 1:4; 2 Peter 2:9,17).

Ah Christians! Christians! I who write, and you who read and hear these things, must not only be spectators of the praise of God's mercy and justice, but parties also, on whom either the infinite mercy or the infinite justice of God shall be everlastingly glorified. But whether of these, I cannot tell, and only God knows. In the name of Christ, "Let us work out our salvation with fear and trembling, for God is a consuming fire," (Philippians 2:12; Hebrews 11:18). Presumptuous sinners who go on impenitently in their sins, shall at length find

---

[6] Bishop Reynolds *of the passions*. Dr. Pearson on the *Apostle's Creed*. Master Baxter's *Saint's Everlasting Rest*, part 3.

their costs, "that they have treasured up wrath to themselves against the day of wrath," (Romans 2:5; James 5:3) and that the justice of God, as well as his mercy, endures forever; none more terrible than God provoked, woe, and again woe to them all, against whom "mercy itself," shall rise up in judgment, "Now consider this, ye that forget God, lest he tear you in pieces, and there be none left to deliver," (Psalm 50:22).

Chapter 6: Application of the Doctrine

Directs you how to apply the great doctrine of man's future eternity, by which you may escape everlasting punishment, and obtain life eternal, after this life is ended.

Having completed the explanation of the doctrine concerning the great state of man's future eternity, I shall in this last chapter apply it to you, and that by way of exhortation to these two duties,

1. Believe it in general, that man's future condition shall be eternal, either in happiness or misery.

2. Provide in particular, for your own future condition, that it may not be miserable, but happy to all eternity.

1. First, believe it in the general, that the condition of all mankind in the world to come, shall be everlasting and endless, either in felicity or misery. Though you cannot see anything beyond the grace with the eyes of your body, yet with the eye of your understanding, through the perspective glass of the Word, and by the grace of faith you may see beyond this

world, "the great prospect of man's eternity in the world to come, both that of glory, and that other torment; and how blessed the one, and how miserable the other:" Here one says that man as a future creature,[1] the eye of his soul looks beyond this life towards eternity; and it is here that faith is described to be the "evidence of things not seen," (Hebrews 11:1). The nature and use of faith is to be, as it were, instead of sight, or to make the unseen and eternal things of hell and heaven, which God has revealed to be in existence, as if our bodily eyes beheld them; therefore, that you may believe this universal received truth, as verily as if you saw it fulfilled, meditate, pray, and confer about it.

1. Meditate on the certainty of this doctrine, "That all mankind at the end of this world shall go in their bodies and souls into an everlasting condition, either of happiness, or misery." Consider that you have as plain places in Scripture, and as strong Scriptural arguments to prove it, as you have to prove any doctrine contained in the Bible, as appears by what has been already said in our second chapter.

Again, consider how that this doctrine has been received for a truth in all ages of the world, not only by

---

[1] Manchester *Comtempl.*

Chapter 6: Application of the Doctrine

the Jews and Christians, but also by Gentiles and heathens; and therefore if you do not believe it, you are worse than infidels and pagans, because they have only the twilight of nature, and you have the clear light of the sacred Scriptures to convince you of its truth, (Matthew 25:46). Although none can have good hope to go to heaven to enjoy that happiness there, which they would not believe here, yet it is to be feared that many go to hell to feel that misery there, which they would not believe here.

2. Pray to God to give you grace to believe it, and by faith to foresee what the Scripture has plainly shown forth; who knows but that the Lord may persuade you of its truth, while you are in prayer to him to incline your hearts to believe it? (Daniel 9:21-22; Matthew 7:7).

3. Confer about it (if needs be) with some able minister of the Gospel, to the end that you may be strengthened and confirmed in your belief of it, (Malachi 2:7; Acts 10:5-6).

One told Bishop Hooper,[2] after he was in Queen Mary's days condemned to be burned, "That life was sweet, and that death was bitter," thinking by this to have dissuaded him from suffering for righteousness'

---

[2] Mr. Clark on the *Life of Bishop Hooper.*

sake. But the good Bishop replied, "The life to come is more sweet, and death to come is more bitter." Surely, such as men's belief is of heaven and life eternal to come, and of hell and everlasting punishment to come, such will be their desires and endeavors to escape the one, and to obtain the other. And this let all men know for certain, "That the wicked shall go away into everlasting punishment, and the righteous into life eternal," at the last day whether the generality of the world do now believe it, yes, or no, (Matthew 25:46).

2. Secondly, we should strive to provide, in particular, for own condition in the world to come, that it may not be miserable, but happy to all eternity.

That you ought first and above all to provide for your own eternal salvation, and that it is rare Christian policy to do so, these places of Scripture fully prove it, "Seek ye first the kingdom of God, and his righteousness, and all these things shall be added unto you," (Matthew 6:33). "Strive to enter in at the strait gate: for many, I say unto you, will seek to enter it, and shall not be able," (Luke 13:24). "Give diligence to make your calling and election sure; for so an entrance shall be ministered unto you abundantly, into the everlasting kingdom of our Lord and Savior Jesus Christ, (2 Peter 1:10-11).

Chapter 6: Application of the Doctrine

Damescene makes mention of a certain country where they choose their king from among the meanest of the people,[3] and (such was their detestable disloyalty), as that on any distaste taken, they would dispose him and banish him into an island into which he feared he should be banished. When this came to pass, the islanders received him with joy, and he lived in plenty among them until his dying day.

If men are so wise and careful to provide for this life, which is but temporal, how prudent and provident should they be, for the life to come, which is eternal?

If any say unto me, "What shall we do that we may escape everlasting punishment, and inherit eternal life?" (Mark 10:17) which is one of the best questions that was ever asked, my answer to it is this; that you may be delivered from everlasting misery, and that you may be provided for life eternal, against the time which your temporal life shall end, and be no more, take these three general directions: learn necessary principles, practice necessary duties, and use necessary means.

1. First, if you would be saved from eternal damnation, and with everlasting salvation, after this life

---

[3] This story is thus cited by Mr. Strode in his *Anatomy of Morality*, p. 118.

is ended, then learn the fundamental principles of the Christian religion, that are most needful to be known to salvation, as suppose those articles of faith, contained in that famous creed commonly called the Apostles' Creed.

But more particularly labor rightly to understand these four principles, which are the first things in the Christian religion that everyone ought to learn, and believe.

1. First, that there is one only living and true God,[4] who is an infinite spirit in being and all perfection, distinguished into three persons, the Father, the Son, and the Holy Spirit, the Maker and Governor of all things, who made man after his own image, in knowledge, righteousness, and holiness, and so in a happy condition, (Genesis 1:27 with Colossians 3:10 and Ephesians 4:24).

2. Secondly, that our first parents, Adam and Eve, sinned eating the forbidden fruit, and thereby fell from their original righteousness, and became dead in sin, and wholly defiled in all the faculties and parts of soul and body.[5] And they being the root of all mankind, the guilt

---

[4] 1 Timothy 2:5; 1 Corinthians 8:4, 6; John 4:24; Matthew 28:19; Genesis 1:1; Psalm 103:19.
[5] Genesis 1:17, 3:6-7; Titus 1:15; Romans 3:10-19; Acts 17:26; Psalm 51:5; Romans 5:11, 18; Ephesians 2:1-2.

Chapter 6: Application of the Doctrine

of their sin was imputed, and the same death in sin and corrupted nature conveyed to all their posterity descending from them by ordinary generation; so as that our first parents by their fall brought themselves and all mankind into a sinful and damnable condition, (Romans 5:12-20; 1 Corinthians 15:21-22).

3. Thirdly, that mankind in this way fallen, being unable to deliver themselves out of the estate of sin and misery, "God so loved the world, that he sent forth his only begotten Son, Jesus Christ,"[6] who was conceived by the Holy Spirit in the womb of the virgin Mary of her substance, and born of her, yet without sin, and so became a man, and was, and continues to be, God and man in two distinct natures, and one person forever. He was made under the law, and was obedient to it, and endured the misery which was due to man for breaking of it. He died for our sins, and suffered for our salvation, and was buried, and rose again the third day, who ascended up into heaven, and sits at the right hand of God, from whence he will come to judge both the quick and the dead, (Acts 10:42).

---

[6] Romans 5:6; 10:3,15; Matthew 1:1; Galatians 4:4; Hebrews 4:15; John 1:14; Luke 1:31; Romans 9:5; Philippians 2:8; 1 Corinthians 15:3-4; Acts 1:9-10; Colossians 3:1.

4. Fourthly, that the Lord requires all people who would be saved through his mercy in Christ to repent of their sins,[7] to believe in his Son Jesus Christ, to live a holy life, and to wait upon him in his own ordinances,[8] as the Word, prayer, and sacraments. And those who by the grace of God sincerely obey these precepts shall be saved, and those who willfully and finally disobey them, shall be damned in their souls after death and particular judgment, and in their bodies also, after the resurrection, and at the general and last judgment, (Mark 16:16; Romans 8:13; Matthew 25:46).

Though these are the main principles that are most needful to be known to salvation, yet I shall mind you not to rest here, but to "read and search the holy Scriptures, which are able to make you wise unto salvation, and perfect unto all good works," (John 5:39; 2 Timothy 3:15-17).

2. Secondly, if you would escape everlasting punishment, and inherit life eternal at the end of this life, then practice the fundamental duties of the Christian religion, that are most necessary to be done to salvation,

---

[7] Matthew 4:17; 1 John 3:23; Titus 2:11-12.
[8] Proverbs 8:32-34; Matthew 7:7; 28:1, 20.

Chapter 6: Application of the Doctrine

which are chiefly these four, in respect of the acts and exercise of saving grace.

1. Repent of all your sins.

2. Believe in the Lord Jesus Christ with all your heart.

3. Live a holy life according to the rule of all God's commandments.

4. Renew your repentance and faith, all the days of your life, as your sins are renewed.

1. First, repent of all your sins, both original and actual. "Repent (our Savior says) for the kingdom of God is at hand;" and again, "I came not to call the righteous, but sinners to repentance," and, "except ye repent, ye shall perish," (Matthew 4:17, 9:13; Luke 13:3).

Now then, that you may truly repent of all your sins, observe these three rules:

1. Search and try your ways,[9] by which you may find out your sins of all sorts; be not too hasty in this duty, but ransack every corner of your heart, and think of your sins until you find them out so far as that you can remember no more: and consider how you have deserved the wrath of God, and the damnation of hell for your

---

[9] Lamentations 3:4; Haggai 1:5, 7; Psalm 38:3-5; Romans 5:23; Galatians 3:10.

sins, so that you may be truly affected, and humbled with the sense of your sinful and miserable condition, (Acts 2:37).

2. Having found out your sins, and considered the wrath and curse of God due to you for them, fall down on your knees and humbly confess your sins to the Lord,[10] and be sorry for them, chiefly as they are contrary to the holy nature and the righteous law of God, and the gracious Gospel of Jesus Christ. Judge yourselves for them, and pray to God in the name of Christ for pardon of them, and power against them, (Luke 11:4).

3. Forsake your wicked ways, and turn from all your sins to God, purposing and endeavoring for time to come to walk with him in all the ways of his commandments, (Ezekiel 18:21-22, 30-31; 1 Thessalonians 1:9).

Next to impenitence, taken heed of late repentance. If I had ten thousand souls (an able divine says[11]) "I would not adventure one of them on a deathbed repentance; therefore, repent now, lest your repentance should be too late. Let this be the day of your sincere conversion, (Deuteronomy 29:18-20; Hebrews 3:7-8).

---

[10] Psalm 95:6; Luke 15:18; 1 John 1:9; Ezekiel 36:31; 2 Corinthians 7:10-11; 1 Corinthians 11:31.
[11] Mr. Calamy in his sermon on Hebrews 11:13.

Chapter 6: Application of the Doctrine

2. Secondly, believe in the Lord Jesus Christ with all your heart, and you shall be saved, "For God so loved the world, that he gave his only begotten Son, that whosoever believeth in him should not perish but have everlasting life," (John 3:16). Bucholcerus did so descant on this text in his last sermon before his death, that he ravished the hearts of his hearers with the greatness of God's love to believers. Surely it cannot be but something that moves the heart of his people, that Christ ever was, and ever will be, the *common salvation* of all believers, (Jude 3).

Therefore that you may believe to life everlasting, endeavor these two things:

1. Endeavor to understand how Christ is offered in the Gospel to sinners, namely to be "Wisdom and righteousness, and sanctification, and redemption, and all in all," (1 Corinthians 1:30; Colossians 3:11). He is offered to all sorts of sinners, who see a need of him, and who are willing to have him jointly together, for these holy and heavenly ends, (Matthew 11:28; John 7:37).

2. Endeavor to receive Christ, (and God in Christ) and to rest on him alone for salvation, as he is offered to you in the Gospel, (John 1:12; Isaiah 26:3-4, 50:10).

Do not say, I must not presume to accept Christ, because my sins are many and great, and I am not humbled enough for them. For truly, truly, Christ had not come to the world, but to save sinners, yes, and the chief of sinners who come to him to be saved.[12] And Christ, who is rich in grace, does not expect to receive anything from poor sinners, but to be received by them, (Revelation 22:17).

Therefore, do not defer your believing or acceptance of Christ,[13] but endeavor to come to him, as God shall draw you, and be willing to close with Christ, and to believe on him, as God shall make you willing. And humbly put yourselves on Christ, and wholly give up yourselves to Christ to be taught, pardoned, sanctified, and saved by him, in his own appointed time and way, and then know for certain, that Christ will in no wise refuse you, but will undertake to be the author of eternal salvation to you, and that God in Christ will be your God and portion forever, (Psalm 73:25-26).

3. Thirdly, live a holy life according to the rule of all God's commandments. For the Scripture says, "That without holiness none shall see the Lord; and that

---

[12] 1 Timothy 1:15; Hebrews 7:25.
[13] Acts 16:30-31; Psalm 103:10; Isaiah 64:7; 2 Corinthians 8:5; John 6:37-39; Hebrews 5:9.

Chapter 6: Application of the Doctrine

godliness hath the promise of the life that now is, and of that which is to come," (1 Timothy 4:8).[14] And again, "That the grace of God which bringeth salvation, doth teach us to deny ungodliness and worldly lusts, and to live soberly, righteously, and godly in this present world," (Titus 2:11-12; 2 Peter 3:11; 1 John 3:3).

For this end, that you may live a holy life, make use of these three helps:

1. Apply by faith the death and resurrection of Christ,[15] and the particular promises of sanctification made to believers in Christ, by which you may be renewed in your whole man after the image of God, and enabled more and more to die to sin, and to live to newness and holiness of life, (Romans 6:4, 6, 14; Galatians 5:24).

2. Observe the sum of the Ten Commandments, which is, to love the Lord your God with all your heart, and with all your soul, and with all your mind, and your neighbor as yourselves.[16] Love thus exercised in sincerity of heart is the fulfilling of the law, and the epitome of a pious life.

---

[14] Matthew 19:17; Hebrews 12:14; 1 Peter 10:15.
[15] Romans 6:4-6, 8; Ezekiel 36:27; Micah 7:19; 2 Corinthians 7:1; Ephesians 4:23, 25.
[16] Matthew 22:37-40; Romans 13:9-10.

3. Know the Ten Commandments by heart,[17] which are the rule of a holy life. So that, your heart being their keeper, you may ever remember to live according to them. Endeavor by degrees in the use of reading, hearing, meditation, and the like means, to understand what sins are forbidden, and what duties are required in every one of the Ten Commandments, for that purpose, that you may eschew the sins forbidden in them,[18] and perform the duties in them which are required. Have a special care to study, and to practice the duties of your relations, and to strive most against your greatest sins, and to watch over your thoughts, words, and ways,[19] out of a holy fear of sinning, and the rather, because your thoughts, words, and actions must be rewarded or punished for all eternity, (Romans 2:6-9; 2 Corinthians 5:10).

Caution: whatsoever you do in the practice of godliness, do all by the rule of God's Word,[20] in the strength of Christ, through the help of his Spirit, to the glory of God, the adorning of the Gospel, the strengthening of your own assurance, and the good

---

[17] Deuteronomy 11:18; Jeremiah 31:33.
[18] Ezekiel 36:27; John 14:15, 23.
[19] Mark 13:35, 37; 1 Peter 1:17.
[20] Galatians 6:16; Philippians 4:13; Romans 8:13; 1 Corinthians 10:13; Titus 2:10; 2 Peter 1:5-11; 1 John 2:3; Matthew 5:16.

Chapter 6: Application of the Doctrine

example of others. And all this out of singular love and thankfulness to God, for his unspeakable love to you in Jesus Christ, (Luke 1:74-75; John 14:15; 2 Corinthians 5:14).

One Symelces, Captain of the Guard to Emperor Adrian, caused this inscription to be set over his tomb,[21] "Here lieth Similis, who saw many years and lived but seven." Let all Christians take special notice of it, that they live in no other way than as becomes the Gospel of Christ while they live on this earth, (Philippians 1:27; Ephesians 2:1-2, 5; 1 Timothy 5:6).

In short, let our conversation be in heaven, let our discourse be on things above, let our thoughts be on our future eternity, and so let us live to God on earth for eternity, as that we may live with God in heaven to eternity, (2 Corinthians 5:14-15; Philippians 3:20; Colossians 3:2).

4. Fourthly, renew your repentance and faith, all the days of your life, as your sins are renewed; which that you may practice these three *particulars:*

1. Commune with your own heart every morning, and consider how, and in what respect you have sinned

---

[21] *Hic jacet similus; cujus atas multorum quidem annorum fuit; vexit anros duntaxat sepem.*

the day or night past, either by commission, or omission, (Psalm 4:4; Haggai 1:5).

2. Having thought of your sins, and manifold failings, repent,[22] and abhor yourselves for them, and beseech God for Christ's sake to forgive them, and to cleanse you from them; and with this, "Remember that you have an advocate with the Father, Jesus Christ the righteous; who is the propitiation for our sins:" and do not be faithless, but believing, (1 John 2:1-2).

3. Resolve with full purpose of heart through the grace of Jesus Christ, to sin no more, lest a worse thing befall you, (Job 34:31-32; John 5:14). Justin Martyr[23] would say, "it is best of all not to sin, and next to that, after sinning, to repent and amend."

3. Thirdly, if you would avoid everlasting misery, and enjoy eternal felicity, after your temporal life is ended, then make use of the outward means and ordinances of God that are necessary to be used to salvation, and especially of these four *following:*

1. Hear the Word of God publicly preached.
2. Pray daily to God everlastingly to save you.

---

[22] Revelation 2:5; Job 42:6; Luke 11:4.
[23] Mr. Clark on the life of Justin Martyr.

Chapter 6: Application of the Doctrine

3. Make use of the two New Testament sacraments of baptism and the Lord's Supper.

4. Obey the ministers of God's Word, who are set over you in the Lord.

1. First, hear the Word of God publicly preached, as generally at all times, when you have opportunity for it; so especially on the Sabbath day; "Hear (the Prophet says) and your soul shall live: who hath ears to hear (our Savior says) let him hear," (Isaiah 55:3; Matthew 13:9).

Again, Christ informs us that "hearing is the one thing needful," (Luke 10:40, Romans 10:14, John 20:31): because not only faith, but also every other grace usually comes by hearing; yes, and is confirmed and increased by hearing, (Acts 14:21-22; 1 Peter 2:2-3).

2. Secondly, pray daily to God in the name of Christ, to deliver you from everlasting punishment, and to bring you to eternal life after this life is ended, (Matthew 6:10, 13; Luke 21:36).

Pray in your hearts with ejaculations to God,[24] pray in secret, pray in your families, pray in public, pray without ceasing, (1 Thessalonians 5:17). Our Savior says, "ask and it shall be given you; seek and ye shall find; knock, and it shall be opened unto you," (Matthew 7:7).

---

[24] 1 Samuel 1:13; Matthew 6:6; Acts 10:2; 1 Corinthians 14:15-16.

And Paul tells us that "whosoever shall call upon the name of the Lord shall be saved," (Romans 10:13).

3. Thirdly, make use of the two New Testament Sacraments, Baptism and the Lord's Supper; which are to continue to the end of the world, (Matthew 28:19-20; 1 Corinthians 11:26).

Make use of your baptism by way of meditation; as sure as you were baptized, so sure you shall be pardoned and saved, if you truly believe in Christ; for baptism is not only a sign, but also a seal of it to all true believers, (Mark 16:16; Romans 4:11).

Again, make use of the Lord's Supper, by your receiving of it, as often as you may be called to it, and prepared for it; and as often as you "receive, do it in remembrance of the Lord's death," (1 Corinthians 11:26) and of the great ends of his death, which was to deliver all those who rightly believe in him from wrath to come, and to purchase a heavenly inheritance for them. As sure as you shall receive Christ by faith in this Sacrament, so sure the blessed benefits of his death and passion shall be confirmed unto you in it, (Matthew 26:28; Romans 4:11).

4. Fourthly, obey the ministers of God's Word, who are set over you in the Lord, and "submit yourselves

Chapter 6: Application of the Doctrine

unto them, for they watch for your souls, as they that must give account, that they may do it with joy, and not with grief," (Hebrews 13:17). Remember what Jesus Christ has said in this case, "He that heareth you, heareth me, and he that despiseth you, despiseth me: and he that despiseth me, despiseth him that sent me," (Luke 10:16). "If ye know these things, happy are ye, if ye do them," (John 13:17); and that you may be blessed in the practice of them, consider these four motives.

1. First consider that if you think of these things so, as to do thereafter, then you may assuredly conclude that you shall escape everlasting punishment, and inherit eternal life at the end of this life. And you may draw your conclusion of assurance, into a Christian syllogism like this, which may serve instead of a use of *examination:*

Those who know those things that make them wise to salvation, who repent of their sins, and believe in Christ, and who sincerely live a holy life, shall not perish, but have everlasting life, the Lord says in his holy Word. But those who follow the aforementioned directions may say, we through grace have learned those things that make us wise to salvation, we repent of our sins, we believe in Christ, and we sincerely desire and endeavor to live a holy life. [25]Therefore, we shall escape everlasting punishment and enjoy eternal life after our temporal life is ended.

And if this is true, how happy will you be, that you were ever born. Consider it, as it is briefly expressed in these Scriptures, "when Christ shall appear, you shall be like him: where he is, there you shall be, that you may behold his glory, and see him as he is, face to face," (John 3:2, 10, 14:3; 1 Corinthians 13:12). "You shall be ever with the Lord, in whose presence is fulness of joy, and at whose right hand there are pleasures forevermore," (1 Thessalonians 4:17; Psalm 16:11); and so be as perfectly happy as you could ever possibly be.

2. Secondly consider that if through carelessness you forget the duties you have been exhorted to, so as finally to neglect them, then you may sadly fear that the Lord shall weigh you in his balance, that you will be found wanting, (Daniel 5:27) and in the number of those who shall be doomed on the last day, to go away into everlasting punishment. And then woe, woe to you, it would have been good for you if you had never been born.

---

[25] John 17:3; Matthew 4:17; John 3:16; Romans 8:13; 1 John 10:2-3, 17.

Chapter 6: Application of the Doctrine

In the fear of God consider the miseries that will come on you at the last day, if you die "without repentance toward God, and without faith toward our Lord Jesus Christ." Seriously think with yourselves, how sad your condition will be, if you are condemned with the wicked of the world, "to depart from the Lord, and from heaven, his dwelling place, and to go into hell, into the fire that never shall be quenched, and into the lake that burneth with fire and brimstone," (Matthew 25:41; Mark 9:43-44; Revelation 21:8).

And now can you escape the damnation of hell, if you walk in the broad way that leads to it, and if you live and die such ignorant and disobedient sinners, as the Lord expressly threatens "to punish with everlasting destruction from his presence, and from the glory of his power?" (2 Thessalonians 1:7-9; Hebrews 2:3).

Some have been moved with fear of hellfire,[26] to cause these words of the Prophet Isaiah, "Who amongst us shall dwell with everlasting burnings," (Isaiah 33:14), to be written in letters of gold over their chimney mantles. O! that you who read and hear these things, would be so moved with fear of hell, and fire eternal, as to begin forthwith to prepare to escape it!

---

[26] *To. Pet. camois b.* in France in his *Draught of Eternity*, Num. 75.

3. Thirdly consider what it is for which you neglect to provide for your own eternal welfare. Is it not either for sin itself, which is altogether evil, or else is it not for the love you bear to this present world, either to the pleasures, riches, or honors of it? All which are but caskets of happiness, and gilded emptiness. Yes, they are not only vain, but vanity itself. "Vanity of vanities, (the preacher says) vanity of vanities, all is vanity," (Ecclesiastes 1:2). And therefore, they are not provisions for a blessed eternity.

And will you venture to neglect the great duties which concern your eternal salvation, either for so vile a thing as sin, or for such vain things as cannot satisfy your immortal souls? God forbid you should do so!

King Lysimachus [27] being constrained through thirst to yield his kingdom to the Scythians for a cup of cold water, when he had drunk it, said, "Oh for what a small pleasure have I parted with my great kingdom?" Whosoever shall lose the eternal good things of the world to come, to gain the temporal good things of this world, will have cause to say, when it is too late, "Oh for how small a matter have I lost the everlasting kingdom of heaven!" For, "What is a man profited (our Savior

---

[27] Plutarch. Apoth.

Chapter 6: Application of the Doctrine

says) if he shall gain the whole world, and lose his own soul? or what shall a man give in exchange for his soul?" (Matthew 16:26). Man's eternal salvation is more worth, yes, infinitely more worth than the whole world.

4. Fourthly, consider that the time of your life is the only time that you have to provide for your eternal condition. If it is not done here, there is no help afterward; for after death comes judgment, and after judgment, eternity, either of comfort or torment, (Ecclesiastes 11:3, Hebrews 9:27).

Aquinas was accustomed to say,[28] "Make much of time in the matter of salvation." And truly you had need to do so, for the work of salvation is great, and the time of your life is short and uncertain, and yet your lifetime (such as it is) is your, "Fair, or market day" for heaven, and your, "seed time," (Galatians 6:7-8) for your harvest in the other world, yes, and the only time that God has lent you to provide for a blessed eternity. If you do not make sure of heaven while you live, it will be out of your reach when you are dead, and then you cannot possibly avoid hell, and everlasting misery, (Luke 16:26).

---

[28] Mr. Clark on the life of Aquinas.

Do not say, it will be time enough hereafter, because you are not sure of that.[29] Sudden deaths are common, and for all you know, you may die a sudden death as ever anyone did, and it may be today before tomorrow. But suppose you should be delivered from sudden death, yet remember that you are going quickly toward the common death of all men, and consequently, towards eternity, either of comfort, or torment. Therefore, what you have to do concerning your eternal salvation, do it speedily, and with all your might, lest death come before you are ready for it, (Ecclesiastes 9:10; John 9:4).

There is a sad story about Caesar Borgias,[30] who said on his sick bed, "While I was in health I provided for everything but death, and now death is come, and I am not provided for it." You may justly fear that this will be your complaint one day, if you presume to put off the great concerns of your everlasting salvation, until sickness or death.

Often consider of your latter end,[31] and how you must hereafter live forever, either in hell or heaven. And seriously think with yourself, if you were to die this day,

---

[29] 2 Corinthians 6:2; Hebrews 3:7-8.
[30] Pilius P. Alexander f. 1490 *Wolfus*.
[31] Deuteronomy 31:19.

into whether of these two places of eternity your soul would go, into hell eternal, or into heaven eternal? And since you know not the day of your death, therefore, pray daily, "Lord Jesus, if I should die this day, then grant that this day my soul may be with thee in paradise, and that my body may be raised at the last day, fashioned like to your glorious body, and reunited to my soul; and that then, I may be ever with you, both in body and soul," (Luke 23:42-43; Philippians 3:21; 1 Thessalonians 4:17).

One of the German princes[32] took for his device, "A candle burning in a candlestick, with this motto, "I serve others, and spend myself; In this undertaking I have spent myself like a burning candle, to give you light, and to do you the best service I can for my life, for the furthering of your eternal salvation."

I hope that the Lord will cause this small treatise to preach effectually when I cannot, and which is more, after I am dead, and entered in my soul into my endless eternity.

And now for a conclusion, I shall be bold to tell you, whoever you are, that read and hear the things contained in this book, that though you know the infallible doctrine of man's future eternity, yet if you do

---

[32] Erastus Dun. Lunehergensin ex philippi loch manlionis.

not live answerable to it, you may be for all that, damned to all eternity. May the Lord have mercy on us for our blessed Savior has said, "Not everyone that saith unto me, Lord, Lord, shall enter into the kingdom of heaven, but he that doth the will of my Father which is in heaven," (Matthew 7:21).

The Italian form of begging is, (as my author tells me) "do good to yourselves."[33] As I have been on my knees to beg God's blessing on my poor labors for you, so I could be content to come on my knees from God to you, to beseech you "to do good to yourselves." For, if you hear and learn, and repent and believe, and walk uprightly, and so be eternally saved, who will have the best of it but yourselves? And if you live and die in ignorance and obedience, and so be everlastingly damned, who is like to have the worst of it, but yourselves?

O! that every reader of this book would think on these things! O! that my beloved parishioners, and worthy friend in Essex would think on these things! O! that my ever dear kindred, and respected countrymen in Lancashire would think on these things! O! that all England would think on these things! O! that all the

---

[33] Gio Torriano p. 51.

Chapter 6: Application of the Doctrine

world would think of these things! O! that all of you, both small and great would[34] remember these things, "That you must all die and go into one of these two eternities, either into everlasting punishment, or into life eternal, in your souls after death, and in your bodies also, after the general resurrection, and the day of judgment; and that the great business you came into this world for is to provide for a blessed eternity in the world to come."

O! that these words were written on some place in your closets or houses, where you might daily see them: or rather, that they were written upon your hearts, that having them in your minds, you might be moved to prepare for your future eternity, by your frequent remembrance of it.

I say once more, O! that all of you would seriously think on these things, and of their infinite importance, not so, as to trouble your heads or hearts with them, but so, as to be moved by them, in time, and in, "this your day," (Luke 19:41), to prepare for your eternal salvation, that as many of you as it is possible, may be kept from perishing everlastingly.

Beloved, my last words to you are to tell you that I can call God and man to record, that I have set before

---

[34] *Memento te esse mortalem; & Annos aternos in menit habe.*

you "the eternal recompenses of hell and heaven, of everlasting punishment and life eternal,"[35] and have shown you the condition of both estates. Behold, I have told you before what is likely to become of you, forever hereafter. And now, to close all this, let me be importunate with you, to make sure work about your everlasting salvation; get it cleared up to you, that Christ is your Lord and Savior, and you are made forever, (John 20:28-29; Philippians 1:21).

What shall I say more? Thoroughly learn the necessary principles, sincerely practice the necessary duties, and diligently use the necessary means that I have exhorted you to, and rather suffer than refuse to do what the Lord has commanded and further others in your calling and place, to do likewise.[36] And then by the grace of God in Christ, you shall not perish but shall have everlasting life, after this life is ended.

Now the most infinitely merciful God, for the infinite merits of Christ, give us grace to do whatever he has commanded, by which we may be delivered from the infinite misery of hell, and by which we may be brought at last to the infinite felicity of heaven, to the glory and

---

[35] Deuteronomy 30:19.
[36] Acts 5:25, 41; 2 Timothy 3:3, 19.

Chapter 6: Application of the Doctrine

honor of his infinite mercy, world without end. Amen and amen.

FINIS

Other Books on Heaven and Hell Published by Puritan Publications

The Way to Escape the Horrible and Eternal Burnings of Hell
by Thomas Vincent (1634–1678)

This book is the last of Thomas Vincent's works, and interestingly enough, the works contained in this volume are on hell. This is a book to give family and friends who need to escape the coming of God's wrath. Also contained in this volume are Vincent's posthumously published "choice sayings" as an appendix.

The Eternity and Certainty of Hell's Torments
by William Strong (d. 1654)

Hell is one of the most dreadful topics, but also one of the most important. 13% of Jesus' teaching was on judgment and hell. This work by Strong is outstanding. Listen to this Westminster Divine on an important subject.

A Treatise on Hell's Terror
by Christopher Love (1618-1651)

Jonathan Edwards said this was one of the best works he'd ever read on the doctrine of hell. I'd have to agree. After reading this work over the years, it is by far one of the top works on hell. Don't let this one pass you by.

Tormenting Tophet: A Description of Hell
by Henry Greenwood (d. 1634)

Henry Greenwood is a gem among puritans, and little known. This, one of his most popular works, is a hard doctrine to study since it pulls on our emotional strings. Hell is doctrine which is indeed awful and dreadful, yet it is of God. It is a dreadful thing, but yet a common thing, for people to go to hell.

Hell with Everlasting Torments Asserted
by Nicholas Chewney (1610-1685)

This work is one of the best manageable treatises that demonstrates the eternal realities of the place of endless punishment: hell. It is one of the few surviving works of Dr. Chewney we have.

Heaven's Glory
by Christopher Love (1618-1651)

What will heaven be like? Love's work is a masterful treatment of Colossians 3:4 showing the glory and happiness prepared for the elect in Christ. This work parallels Love's book, "Hell's Terror".

Christ's Ascension and Second Coming from Heaven
by Christopher Love (1618-1651)

Are you ready for him to return from heaven? This wonderful work on eschatology by Christopher Love not only combats the impossibility of the 1000-year reign of Christ on the earth, but especially comforts believers in the immanent reality of Jesus' return from heaven.

The Way to Heaven
by John Philips (1585-1663)

There is no salvation outside the church. Philips explains why this is so important, and every Christian should understand why God has ordained the specific means of salvation through the church in order to bring in his elect through his one and Only Son. A masterful work following the teaching of the bible and the doctrines around ecclesiology.

Taking Hold of Eternal Life in Christ
by George Gifford (1547-1620)

Is holiness of life a necessary prerequisite for getting into heaven? Do you have the power as a Christian to overcome sin? What has Jesus Christ done in enabling you to live righteously according to his commandments? How do you successfully glorify Jesus Christ in your daily walk?

www.ingramcontent.com/pod-product-compliance
Lightning Source LLC
Chambersburg PA
CBHW070207100426
42743CB00013B/3079